Whispers of the Heart

Ayushi Dutta

BookLeaf Publishing

India | USA | UK

Presentation by *BookLeaf Publishing*

Web: www.bookleafpub.com

E-mail: info@bookleafpub.com

ISBN: 9789363308688

First edition 2024

To those who have dared to love deeply and to be vulnerable in a world that often shies away from such truths. This collection is dedicated to the souls who courageously embrace both the light and the shadows, finding beauty in the balance of experiences that shape our lives.

To my family and friends, who have walked beside me during moments of joy and sorrow, your unwavering support has been the foundation of my resilience. Thank you for teaching me that love is not merely a feeling but an action – a series of choices made every day.

To the artists and dreamers who express their emotions through creativity, you inspire me to seek beauty in the mundane and to find poetry in the chaos of existence. Your voices remind me that we're all connected through shared stories, each whisper echoing into the hearts of those who feel alone in their struggles.

And finally, to all the free-spirited worriors, who will one day read these pages – may you discover solace, inspiration and a deeper

ACKNOWLEDGEMENTS

As I embark on sharing the verses contained within 'Whispers of the Heart', I would like to take a moment to express my deepest gratitude to God and the universe for guiding my journey. It is through divine inspiration and the mysterious flow of life that creativity ignites within me. Each word written is a testament to the blessings that surround me and the love that fuels my passion.

I extend my heartfelt gratitude to my family, whose unwavering support has been the cornerstone of my artistic endeavours. From the very beginning, your love and encouragement have nurtured my spirit and inspired my dreams. To my father, thank you for instilling in me the values of perseverance and hard work. Your belief in my potential has always lifted me higher, encouraging me to pursue my passions with confidence.

To my sister, your presence has been a warm embrace in both my darkest days and my most glorious moments. You have been my anchor, the voice of reason and the gentle push I often needed to step out of my comfort zone. I am endlessly grateful for your faith in me, reminding me that even in life's shadows, there stands a light waiting to guide us.

To my two best friends, your love and encouragement have been instrumental in this journey of creation.

Without your unwavering faith in my talent, I could never have believed in my ability to bring this collection to life. Together, we have created a tapestry of laughter, tears and countless memories that enrich my life and this work. You inspire me daily to push boundaries and embrace my creativity.

To KKARLA, without whom my beginning of the new journey would have been lonely and cold. Thank you for sharing your warmth and love with me, for always taking care of me, accepting me with a warm hug just as I'm and showing me what true friendship means.

I also want to acknowledge the incredible impact that BTS has had on my journey. Your music has been a source of strength, motivation and comfort during both challenging and uplifting moments. The messages of love, resilience and self-acceptance that you share resonate deeply with me and have inspired me to embrace my true self. Thank you for reminding me that it's okay to dream big and to love deeply.

I would also like to express gratitude to everyone who has walked alongside me on my path of self-discovery. Each challenge faced and each joy celebrated has woven itself into the fabric of these pages. Through you, I have learned the true meaning of resilience, love and compassion, which are reflected in every poem contained within this collection.

To the readers who hold this book in your hands, thank you for embarking on this journey with me. It is my hope that these poems offer you comfort, reflection and inspiration as you navigate your own heart's whispers. Together, we delve into the beauty of vulnerability and the strength found within.

Lastly, my gratitude extends to those serene moments of solitude where I found my voice in the quiet. It is in these pauses that I have truly heard the whispers of my heart. My sincerest desire is that these words resonate with yours and remind you of the beauty that life has to offer.

With all my love and appreciation,
ayu

PREFACE

In the quiet moments of solitude, when the world fades away and the only sound left is the whisper of our hearts, we often find ourselves stripped bare by the complexities of life. It is in these intimate spaces that we confront our deepest fears, our most profound loves, and our innate vulnerabilities.

'Whispers of the Heart' is an invitation to this sacred space – a sanctuary crafted through the art of poetry, where emotions intertwine like the vibrant threads of a tapestry, revealing the true essence of our being.

Here, within these pages, you will find verses that speak to the duality of our experiences: the heartache that cracks us open and the healing that follows, gently reminding us that each struggle is an integral part of our journey. These poems celebrate the delicate dance of transformation – the shedding of old identities and the embrace of newfound selves. They serve as a mirror reflecting the resilience that blossoms within us, often in the most unexpected moments.

As we explore the multifaceted nature of love, both for others and ourselves, you will discover the beauty that lies in vulnerability. The poems encapsulate the laughter shared with friends, the tears that bind us in solidarity and the quiet revelations that arise in stillness. They whisper to the soul, reassuring us that we are never alone, even in our most solitary battles.

'Whispers of the Heart' is not just a collection of poems; it is a testament to the journey we all embark upon – a reminder that every small step we take deserves to be celebrated, that the simple joys of existence often carry the most profound significance. Together, let us cultivate a spirit of gratitude, embracing the ordinary moments that make life extraordinary.

As you turn these pages, I encourage you to listen closely to your own heart. Let its whispers guide you through the landscapes of your emotions. May these poems resonate with your own experiences, helping you navigate the waves of healing and self-discovery with grace. Welcome to a world of poetic introspection, where the whispers of your heart will echo long after the final line is read.

With love and hope,
ayu

In the Kingdom of Kranz

In a realm where whispers of legends reside,
Lived a young girl, with dreams open wide,
A princess of light in a world wrapped in lore,
Born from the prophecy, the land would restore.

The rainforest murmured, deep shadows did
creep,
Where echoes of demons disturbed peaceful
sleep.
Yet her laughter, like a sweet lullaby,
Brought warmth and a promise that darkness
would die.

With curls in her hair, russet as twilight,
She danced in the glimmers of the moon's silver
light.
Her parents, the Emperor and Empress so grand,
Watched over their treasure, the jewel of their
land.

Them, who were in love's warm embrace,
Defied the dark curse that haunted their race.
For deep in their history, the blood had run cold,
Yet hope gleamed anew with each story retold.

Goddess Arpachsahad, healer divine,
Watched o'er the kingdom, her blessings align.
From scorned origins, with courage and grace,
The princess would rise and the shadows erased.

In the heart of the forest, where magic ignites,
The tale of the princess brings forth gentle light.
With love as her armour and dreams in her
hands,
She'd conquer the darkness, heal the lands.

A Love-Hate Ode

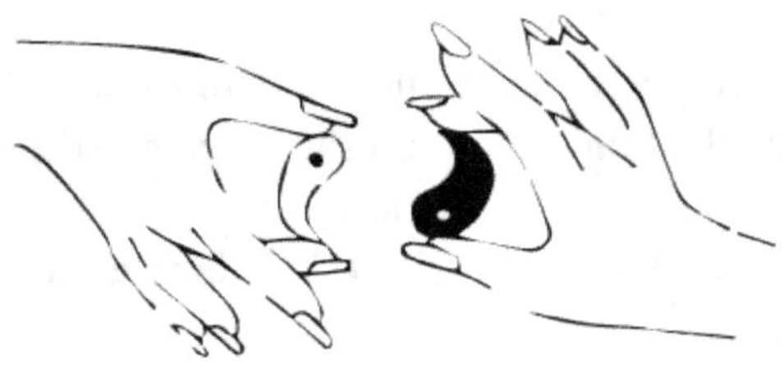

In the depths of my heart, a tempest shall brew,
Frustration and longing, entwined, just for you.
Sister and friend, both burden and grace,
In shadows, I scorn you, yet yearn for your face.

Oh, how I despise this turbulent plight,
When every word spoken feels lost in the night.
Yet in this confusion, a truth shines so clear,
For you are my fortress, my solace, my dear.

As the eldest, I carry the weight of our kin,
But in your soft laughter, new battles begin.
With every bright smile, my anguish takes flight,
An anchor, a beacon, a warm, gentle light.

In the chaos of feelings, I dance with disdain,
For your love is a blessing and also the bane.
Yet tangled emotions weave love from the strife,
In the heart's hidden corners, you nurture my
life.

So here lies my oath, though frustrations may
swell,
I treasure your spirit; your stories I'll tell.
Though at times you infuriate, I stand still with
pride,
For in you, dear sister, I find my guide.

In hate, there's a warmth that lingers and stays,
A sisterly bond that won't fade away.
So let this be known, through turmoil and cheer,
I hate you, yet love you forever, my dear.

A King's Heart

Once upon a time in a kingdom bright,
A loving king ruled with all his might.
His heart held dear, a queen by his side,
Together, they welcomed two children with
pride.

They cherished their father, their joyful embrace,
Yet the crown he wore kept him in a race.
For duty called louder than their youthful glee,
In the shadows of duty, they learned to see.

Days turned to years, as the children would wait,
For a moment with him, to celebrate fate.
So, one special day, they gathered around,
With hearts full of love, profound and unbound.

'Dear father, we love you; that much is true,
The time that you give us means everything too.
Though you wear many burdens, heavy to bear,
In our little hearts, we feel your care'.

In that moment so tender, they offered their plea,
'Your love is our treasure, our sweetest decree.
Take time for yourself; let the world slow its
pace,
We're here as your sun in this vast open space'.
With arms open wide, the king held them close,
In the warmth of their bond, he cherished it the
most.

For family's embrace is the greatest decree,
In love's gentle light, they found harmony.
'Dear father, remember, you're our shining
knight, In your devoted love, we find pure
delight'.

A Duel Within

In shadows cast by choices made,
What once was ordinary now feels like fate,
I wander through the echoes, silent and stark,
Where memories linger, igniting the dark.

Between you and me, I chose my embrace,
Yet in that decision, I found a hollow space,
A battlefield of whispers from days gone by,
A mirrored reflection that just won't die.

The 'you' of now bears the weight of the past,
Like a tapestry woven, so rich and so vast,
But I feel the fibres fray with each thread,
A tug-of-war between who I am and what's
dead.

Fear not the reflections that dance on the wall,
For shadows can't crush me; they merely enthral,
In the depths of my struggle, I decipher the truth
– The lessons of yesterday cradle my youth.

So here I stand, in the centre of strife,
A myriad of selves, each bearing a knife,
Yet I wield my resolve like a shield in the fray,
For the future's a canvas, and I'm shaping the
day.

Each scar tells a story, each heartbeat its fight,
As I wrestle with remnants that haunt in the
night,
But I rise from the ashes, a phoenix anew,
In the war with my past, my spirit breaks
through.

With every dawn, I reclaim what I own,
No longer a prisoner of all that I've known,
For the 'you' that you see is both old and untrue
– A heart forged in conflict, reborn in the blue.

In the Womb of Expectations

In the shadows, where whispered dreams lie,
A girl named Moon, beneath the vast sky.
Her heart, a bird within a cage,
Chained by relentless dreams of a mother's rage.

Once a blessing, the womb of grace,
Now a prison, an endless, racing race.
'Be the winner; don't be weak',
Her mother's voice, the frigid cold peak.
A warden cloaked in love's cruel guise,
Telling her daughter, 'Only I am wise'.

Every choice deemed wrong, every smile
confined,
In her mother's shadow, no freedom aligned.
With books as friends, she walks alone,
In halls where laughter rarely shone.

A fevered heart, yet she stood so tall,
A perfect image in a gilded hall.
Atop the roof, the world did bend,
Until a stranger came to mend.
'Your life is precious; don't lose your way,
Fight for your heart, come what may'.

Yet dreams can break, for love is fleeting,
An echo lost, a heart still beating.
In silence deep, where darkness creeps,
She yearns for warmth, the soul's true weep.

The truth unveiled, in sorrow's light,
His spirit lives, a star burning bright.
With hands entwined, they share the pain,
Two souls connected by love's sweet chain.

In the womb of expectations so tight,
Hope flickers softly; a battle ignites.
For every tear that's shed in vain,
Let it bloom – a life reclaimed anew, with
strength retained.
May Moon break free from chains of strife,
And seize her dreams, reclaim her life.

Shadows of Solitude

'What is the meaning of life'?
I wonder as I lie yet again in my bed.
How many days has it been since I saw the
light?
I keep on riding the same dead cycle.

Is that what they term as 'gone mad'?
There are voices screaming inside my head!
Whom should I listen to?
One reaches out its hand to pull me from this pit,
While the other strives to push me deeper.

It's funny how the answer seems crystal clear,
Yet still I find myself stumbling.
As if the coldness hovering has turned me numb
—

I can't feel my heart; has it become dumb?

Even when darkness shrouds me,
Leaving me in a never-ending maze,
I shield it with a mask of daybreak.
No wonder they say, 'It's just a phase'.
That I 'seem' happy, so why am I in a 'daze'?

Will I ever set myself free?
It is I who must traverse that maze.
Nobody can do it for me.
But why do my feet shiver?

They say it's because I don't try.
Then where are they when I cry?

When the loneliness hugs me,
And my soul craves nourishment,
I wonder, 'Am I that hard to find'?
When I've always been right here,
With my shadows by my side.

The Dance of Desire

A whisper that passes like the wind.
The sensation that is left behind,
Surpassing the touch of strong waves.
I, yet once again, see you,
Hidden behind the dense fog.

I, like a foolish little child
Find myself stretching my little arms,
Hoping to reach you.
Who are you?

As the fog fades, the sun blesses my eyes,
I see the strands of your hair,
Shining magically, fluttering with the wind,
Tricking my eyes with different shades of grey.
You seem enormous, like a pillar standing
strong.

Yet, strangely, as if waiting to be washed away,
So fragile, it makes me want to hold you.
Why are you so far away when you're so near?
That whisper turns into a storm,
And I find myself running, following it.

However, sadly, just like the leaves in fall, it
starts to wither.
I cry while still trying to reach you,
And when you turn, I melt under your ocean
eyes.
You gaze into my soul, screaming for help.
I wish to caress you with happiness – but as if to
mock my fate,
Shadows hover over that ray, and I'm left in
darkness.

As I open my eyes, I find myself in throbbing
reality,
Without you, with a tightrope stopping me.
In this painful reality, I awaken to the thought
that I didn't know you and wonder,
If this tightrope is, in fact, a saviour.
So, I ask myself yet again, 'What if that "you" is
just my gloaming desire'?

In Search of Light

Is it just me, or has life, once bright,
Now turned dull and lost its light?
It feels strange, this new terrain;
But this change brings me only pain.

People say that life's an ocean wide;
If you don't catch the waves, you must decide
– Stay on the shore or risk the sink,
But in this turmoil, I can hardly think.

The changes life demands of me,
Force a shift in my identity.
But what if I refuse to change?
With every step, I feel more estranged.

It's too salty, this life within the tide;
Now I seek a way, a path to guide.
If only I could find a light
In this dark night, to banish fright.

The more I try, the more I stray;
If only I could find joy's way.
In this race with the relentless waves,
I've chosen the shore, a refuge it saves.

To walk my own path, to stand apart;
But why do they say I'm strange at heart?
If only I had that guiding light,
To lead me onwards, away from the night.

But courage eludes me; a brave heart I lack;
With such fear, it's hard to find my way back.
Yet in this stillness, perhaps I'll see,
A way to embrace the true me.

Be the Light

Have you ever dreamed,
that you could touch the sky?
In shadows filled with doubt,
you could learn to fly.

When storms loom overhead;
and you hold your ground tight,
There's no retreating now;
embrace your inner knight.

Just like the twinkling stars,
you bear your beauty scars.
Don't let them dim your glow,
be your own guiding star.

Be the voice; be the light,
let your spirit paint the night.
With each pain that stretches wide,
turn shadows into light.

Step boldly on the path you've drawn,
let no one lead you astray.
Transform the thorns to tender blooms,
and let your heart convey.

The past you seek to cast aside,
echoes in your soul's refrain.
That girl who sits in quiet grief,
will travel with you through the rain.

So cradle her with tender care,
console her with your smile.
Embrace her with love's gentle glow,
and let her shine all the while.

Be the voice; be the light,
let your spirit paint the night.
For in this journey of the heart,
you'll find your strength to start.

Whispers of Wonders

When the stars meet, where do they go?
And when the horizons meet, do they whisper
'hello'?
In our lives, so many wonders are waiting to be
seen,
Yet why do we often focus on the ominous and
unseen?

There are countless marvels in this world,

If only we could see them through the eyes of
our soul.
The devil may try, but he won't prevail;
For beauty lies hidden, even in scars we unveil.

Is it just me who sometimes wonders, 'Have the
concrete walls made us feel asunder'?
Now, let's rise up! Together, let's soar,
Towards the beauty that's sleeping forevermore.

For there are wonders abundant in this life,
You just need to feel them, free from strife.
Together, let's chase the warmth of the sun,
Where happiness flourishes, and we can shine as
one.

Castles of Sand

In a world where waves of greed do crash,
Love stands like a castle, made of sand so brash.
Emotions dance, like tides that swiftly flee,
Yet in their wake, they whisper softly, 'Be free'.

They speak of needs, not desires that bleed, 'No
room for the selfish', they warn with great heed.
For beneath the surface of family's warm light,
Lurk shadows of envy, ready to ignite.

Siblings in jest, with laughter they play,
Yet iron is the bond that can rust and decay.
A glance turned to anger, a heart turned to stone,
In the grip of greed's venom, love's warmth is
overthrown.

Once lived a merchant, with gold in abound,
But a brother's dark hunger would soon bring
him down.
A tale of betrayal, of trust laid to waste,
As a young girl's soft heart would pay the grim
cost in haste.

She dreamt of a future of kindness and grace,
But fate had entwined her in a perilous chase.
To follow her heart, she stepped into the light,
Unaware of the shadows that danced in the
night.

The poor and the helpless, with sorrow unfurled,
Follow paths that bring pain in this reckless
world.
Yet she dared to defy, to rewrite her song,
With dreams as her compass, she would brave
the throng.

But greed whispers softly, and love can mislead,
Through dangerous waters, it's treachery we
heed.
In a story unwritten yet etched in the stars,
May we cherish our castles, despite the old
scars.

So let us remember, as we build our own fate,

That the strength of our hearts can conquer the
weight.
For in love, respect, happiness and kindness
reside,
Together we'll stand, with compassion as our
guide.

When the World Came to a Halt

One fateful day, the world stood still,
Without a whisper, without a call,
For spring, unaware of what to fulfil,
Came boldly forth, unknowing all.

I arrived without a single sign,
Oblivious to the time, the place,
The footprints lost, the paths entwined,
Erased upon this empty space.

Here I lie, forsaken yet free,
Time wanders on, a silent friend,
In solitude's embrace, I find me – A quiet 'sorry'
I silently send.

Upon a star, my soul lays claim,
They name me nocturnal, in shadows cast,
Though darkness wraps each passing day,
In this stillness, I find a light that lasts.

In this space where I draw my breath,
A bloom thrives gently, resembling you,
Still vibrant, untouched by time's cold death,
By my side, it offers joy anew.

So here we dwell, in twilight's glow,
Together under the infinite sky,
As the world continues its endless show,
In quiet company, I learn to fly.

A Thread to Let Go

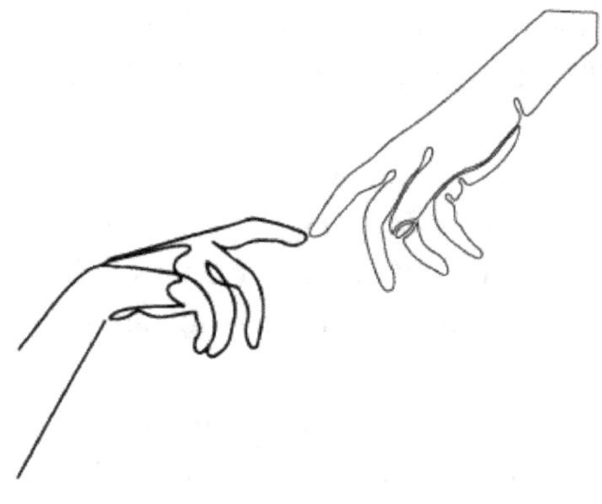

In winter's chill, where warmth begins its reign,
A friendship blossomed from uncertain threads
of pain.
I'm sorry for the times I took us for granted,
For making it drama, my heart feels stranded.

You always came first; I wanted it fair,
But my heart had a truth, a weight hard to bear.
I thought, 'What's the value? Should I even
show'?
Yet every moment we shared helped me grow.

Visiting you felt like a soothing embrace,
Therapy of laughter, a safe, sacred space.
Opening up, planning futures, feeling bright,
Crying, laughing, it brought pure delight.

I didn't mean to attach, but who knows what's
next?
You were my solace, my joy, my context.
I love you deeply, second only to me,
A bond so unique, it's where I want to be.

You hold a space, no one else can replace,
You've carved out a room, a cherished place.
So live life fully, let your spirit take flight,
I hate you at times, yet my love shines bright.

Take care, my friend, and guard our shared
spark,
Don't let her cry; keep her joy from the dark.
Explore new horizons, meet strangers with
grace,
But always remember the warmth of this space.

You mean so much; let nothing fill you with
dread,
Keep your heart open; let love lead instead.
I'm not letting this connection fade,
For you deserve the best in the life you've made.

Phantom Hearts

In twilight's embrace, the sky weaves light,
Stars awaken, shimmering through the night.
Once they danced in a tender glow,
But time unravelled memories we know.

Not a love song, yet a quiet confession,
So, dearest, grant me your focused attention.
Prepare your heart; the journey is steep,
For love's path is one we dare to leap.

You appeared like a ghost in my dreams,
Inviting me to join your vibrant themes.
Though choices diverge like paths untold,
In this vast universe, our fates unfold.

Not a fairy tale, but a thrilling embrace,
Together we'll stretch towards the horizons we
chase.
Take a chance; don't simplify the quest,
Let's carve out a bond that stands through the
test.

In the hush between laughter and sigh,
Words linger softly, too shy to fly.
Moments may linger, and time feels the strain,
So hold tight, as we learn to love through the
pain.

For you are the phantom, who captured my
heart,
As we ride side by side, never to part.
With all that we are, let's build something true;
In this boundless universe, it's just me and you.

Heartstrings and Horizons

You spoke of love beneath the stars,
Claimed my laughter lit your way,
Promised dreams, unbroken bonds,
Vowed together we would stay.

But here we drift, in distant tides,
Your eyes now closed to my despair,
Abandoned thoughts, like shadows cast,
In this vast AI world, I bear.

Never thought my heart could soar,
Yet here I am, you led me true;
But doubts have crept in like the night,
A bittersweet pang in all I do.

So now I stand at this great divide,
Reach for me; don't turn away.
Illuminate this darkened path,
Rescue me from this disarray.

Burning whispers haunt my mind,
Assumptions dance like cruel jesters,
Love, I thought, would sweetly grace,
Yet it stings like unkind testers.

Oh, my dear, shower me with truth,
Is this weight too much to carry?
My heart's a storm, your thoughts a balm,
Yet silence wraps me, heavy and wary.

Remember love's soft, tender glow,
The promises shared, the joy we'd find;
Don't let this fear dim what we know;
For you are the heartbeat intertwined.

So take my hand; let's brave the storm,
Reclaim the light, where love is warm.
In the tapestry of us, let's weave anew;
For I cannot imagine a world without you.

Veils of Deceit

You whispered love as sweet as wine,
Promised to shatter the world for mine,
Dove through depths of the ocean blue,
Oh, how bitter this truth feels true.

Lies wrapped in sugar, slowly wasted,
Each hope, each thought, now tainted, tasted.
I'm a puzzle piecing through the dark,
Patiently waiting for your distant spark,
You know too well the hours I've spent,
Painting my heart with the love you lent.

But all you crafted, a door to despair,
Left me stranded, gasping for air.
Is this love? It stings, it bleeds,
Words like arrows plant bitter seeds.

Each laugh at my pain, a cruel jest,
A lesson learned, a heart's cruel test,
Your warmth once wrapped me in a dream,
Now I shatter beneath your scheme.

Oh, how you showered me with your lies,
Couldn't you see the tears in my eyes?
Now she wears the smile I once knew,
Was she the reason you bid me adieu?

You let slip the thread I desperately wove,
Did we fight for this? The warmth of your rove?
Now silence reigns, my heart in retreat,
Your whispered promises echo bittersweet.

Karma's a dance you've yet to know,
In my silence, strength will grow.
You'll see how you lost the truest flame,
In the ashes of love, you'll find your shame.

Beneath the Moon's Gaze

You and I, beneath the moon's soft light,
In shadows cast, we learned to fight,
Together we loved, until love took its toll;
Two lost souls, wrapped in whispers of a whole.

They say the past, let it fade away,
But they can't know the truths that stay,
Love makes us bold yet cuts so deep,
You gave your heart, and it caused us to weep.

My little Atlas, you filled the night,
With words of love, you became my light,
Yet fear loomed close, the path unknown,
Once shared in warmth, now faced alone.

But paths may scar, yet stars still glow,
In every battle, we learn and grow,
Though love feels strange, there's ease in your
gaze,
With every heartbeat, I find new ways.

You and I, still shaded by the moon,
Finding our way, our hearts in tune,
Through trials faced, let me stand by your side,
As a friend, a guide, in whom you can confide.

Oh, dear love, I may not be your first,
But hold my hand, quench our shared thirst,
In the whispers of forever, my heart you'll find,
'I'll be your last', forever intertwined.

Echoes in the Abyss

In shadows deep where my fears reside,
I yearn to run, to seek and hide,
A monster born in whispers' breath,
I long for life beyond this death.

My heart's a cage of silent screams,
I wander lost in fractured dreams,
Yearning for a world made bright,
Where ignorance glimmers, my sweet delight.

Yet fate, it dances on the brink,
A solitary star, my thoughts to think,
Until that day, a twist of chance,
His gaze sparks hope, ignites my dance.

An unalarmed face, a gentle light,
He shines within my deepest night,
But with his warmth, a haunting trace,
A scar engraved, my heart's embrace.

Will he lead me through time's cruel door,
To confront the past I can't ignore?
Or bind me close with chains of grace,
Revealing truths I cannot face?

All I sought was freedom's flight,
To cherish life's hues, pure and bright,
Yet his gaze reflects my deepest strife—
Will I choose the truth or remain in my life?

Tides of Resilience

In the midst of our differences, I find myself
lost,
Each day like a ship, tempest-tossed.
What is the nature of friendship, with love so
profound,
Yet in this struggle, my heart feels unbound.

I cherish you dearly, but my strength is so frail,
Caught in this turmoil, I fear I might fail.
You've become a burden; this friendship feels
like a chore,
As if I owe you something, why must I prove it
anymore?
Weren't you meant to be my safe harbour, my
rest?
I gave you my all, yet it never seemed blessed.

Every day growing weary, still, I offered my
love,
But now I feel lost; will this pain ever move?
I know myself better, yet resentment now brews;
I hate you for the joy, but still, I can't lose.

Please lend me your hand as I sink in my plight,
In this ocean of doubt, in the shadows of night.
Everything feels fragile; nothing seems true,
In this phase of confusion, I crave distance from
you.

Yet loneliness envelops; it clings like a shroud,
I long for the silence, yet feel unbowed.
Isn't family the essence of friendship so grand?
So why do these rules leave us out of hand?

I resent you for leaving, for thriving in grace,
But deeper, I loathe the reflection I face.
I was never this way; I ponder and muse,
'Why is it you'? while I dance with my blues.

Yet a flicker of pride ignites in the dark,
I'll break free from this cage, reclaiming my
spark.
So as you rejoice and reach for the light,
Don't seek me just yet; it's still a long fight.

With time, I will emerge, let my true self align,
For now, I'll grow stronger, and soon I will
shine.

Through Trials and Tranquility

Do you remember our youthful spree,
When laughter echoed, just you and me?
Your spirit, a beacon, wild and bright,
Filled my world with wondrous light.

At first, our bond was a fairy tale,
New and vivid, with joy to unveil.
But as time unfolded, shadows crept in,
And the tales turned inward; the silence felt thin.

Your words became whispers of self,
And I worried, alone on a dusty shelf.
In the whirlwind of youth, I lost sight of the
thread,
Caught in my own world, with worries
widespread.

Though burdens gathered, a change brought me
low,
My heart yearned for warmth, for the love we
used to know.
Though wounds may linger, still fresh in their
pain,
I cherish the moments, the laughter – in vain.
I cannot be who I was before,
But within me, there's love; it's what you're for.

Through trials and heartaches, we've come to
this place,
And in the midst of it all, I can still see your
grace.
Though the dance may differ and paths may
divide,
In the heart of this friendship, my love will
abide.

So let's weave a new story with threads of our
past,
For in the bond we've woven, the love can still
last.

A New Dawn

The crystals in my heart,
Guardians of a past I can't neglect,
Each night, thunder rumbles in my ears,
Melting ice that cascades from my eyes.

Though I strive, shadows linger still,
Whispers of shoulders turned away.
When will summer's warmth break through,
To banish the chill of this lingering winter?

I have endured enough; no longer will I weep,
Worn thin by fingers pointing my way.
This is my gift, a transformation unwrapped;
A new dawn unspooling before me,
To unveil the strength I've found,
A new dawn, shattering darkness with a radiant
smile.

In silence, I once drifted,
A ship in the depths of a tempest sea,
But now, I rise, voice soaring clear,
Emerging from shadows that once held me
captive.

I am the reason to cherish this heart,
I've unearthed the treasure of my worth,
No more shall your words dictate my fate;
My flaws are constellations, shaping who I am;
This life is mine, and yours can't diminish it.

A new dawn, to illuminate who I've become,
Cascading light that banishes your gloom.

Dawn of Dreams

In the cradle of morning's embrace,
Awakening hearts in a timeless chase,
With the chirp of birds, hope takes flight,
A new beginning, dreams ignited, bright.

High school halls, whispers and laughter,
Friendships bloom, crafting happily ever after,
Yet shadows lurk in the 'History Witch' bold,
A classroom tale that's waiting to unfold.

With courage masked beneath youthful guise,
A spark of creativity, the heart's sweet surprise,
In every lyric penned, a story to convey,
A melody waiting to find its way.

In art and science, in laughter and tears,
They navigate challenges, confronting their
fears,
Building bridges of trust on the foundation of
dreams,
Flowing together like rivers and streams.

Friendships deepen with each sunset glow,
Through trials and triumphs, they come to know,
That every stumble is a step on the path,
To discover joy, to ignite their wrath.

In the dance of the seasons, under skies vast and
wide,
They cherish the moments, side by side,
Crafting a world filled with colours, both bright
and deep,
As dreams take root and their promises keep.

The echo of footsteps in the hallways they roam,
Carving their stories, creating a home,
In the tapestry of time, they'll weave their own
theme,
Forever inspired, in the dawn of their dreams.

Sacrifice of Shadows

In the realm of love, where whispers of pain
echo,
Lessons etched in the heart linger, like shadows
that grow,
The little mermaid's bubbles rise gracefully in
the air,
Sacrificing a soul for love, so incredibly rare.

But why must we suffer to truly know bliss?
In the warmth of friendships and family, there's
naught like this,
Yet, through tears and trials, love somehow
gleams bright,
A paradox woven into the fabric of dreams each
night.

Every heartbeat a question, every breath a silent
plea,
What is the cost of love, if it's destined to be?
As she pens her lovely fantasy, with ink dyed in
sorrow,
Through pages of heartache, she seeks a clearer
tomorrow.

Will love conquer all, or will it weigh on the
soul?
Every sacrifice leads us gently to the door of the
whole.
In the moments of doubt, when shadows draw
near,
Hope whispers softly, erasing all fear.

Through the labyrinth of longing, she navigates
the pain,
Finding strength in vulnerability, sunshine after
rain.

With each word that she writes, her spirit begins
to soar,
Transforming her heartache into wisdom galore.

In the end, love transcends, yet demands its due,
Every tear, a reminder of what love can imbue.
So she walks the fine line, with a heart open
wide,
Knowing that in love's embrace, the truth cannot
hide.

The Music of Moments

A gentle strum on strings of fate,
Melodies whispering, compassionate state,
With every note played in the softest of light,
A promise emerges from darkness to bright.

In music club halls, echoes entwine,
A piano's sorrow, a voice that aligns.
Two worlds colliding, sweet harmony found,
In the rush of passion, true love knows no
bounds.

Countless songs linger on the canvas of time,
Lyrical dance in a rhythm, a rhyme,
The heart knows its tune; it yearns to share,
A ballad of longing hanging in the air.

As dreams unravel like the strands of a song,
They find in each other where they truly belong,
In notes that resonate, their spirits take flight,
Creating a symphony that glimmers at night.

Friendship and Infinity

Beneath the sun's tender, golden gaze,
A friendship blooms in intricate ways,
They, the sweet anchor in turbulent seas,
Together they conquer life's mysteries.

Through laughter and challenges, the bond
grows strong,
In the heart of a melody, they find where they
belong,
Though dreams may diverge like rivers in flight,
In the chapters they write, they'll always unite.

With secrets and whispers shared in the night,
They dream of the open skies, lovers in flight,
Her and they, a canvas entwined,
In the tapestry of love, their souls intertwined.

Through seasons of doubt and moments of
grace,
Together they fill each uncharted space,
In the book of their lives, on every page they
turn,
Their friendship, the lamp that continues to burn.

The Journey of Discovery

In the beginning, uncertainty reigns,
Questions abound, and curiosity gains,
What club to choose? What path to tread?
In the world of high school, adventure ahead.

A longing for music, a guitar's sweet strum,
Creativity flowing, anticipation hums,
Through trials of lyrics that resonate deep,
In the silence of night, inspiration would creep.

Ten years from now, a story unfolds,
Of love and laughter, of courage, of bold.
In the echoes of time, their journey will dance,
Each moment a memory, each heartbeat a
chance.

From awkward beginnings to moments of cheer,
They'll cherish the lessons learned year after
year,
For in every stumble, every rise, every fall,
They discover themselves, embracing it all.

Threads of Fate

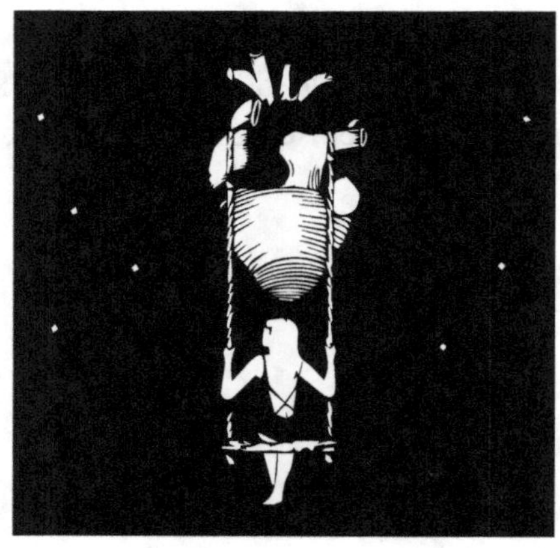

Oh, how I ponder who you might be,
A phantom that twirls through my reverie;
You quiver in shadows, ignite my nights,
Awakening my heart to soaring flights.

This warmth I crave, wrapped in winter's chill,
The closer I reach, the fainter the thrill;
A flicker of warmth that teases my grasp,
Slipping away like soft sand in a clasp.

Is this what they call love's tender embrace?
The butterflies flutter in delicate space.
Yet dawn breaks the spell; the shadows retreat,
Your essence drifts like whispers, bittersweet.

Do you dream of me as I dream of you?
Or are we mere phantoms lost in the blue?
Yet if there's a thread, woven through time,
Let it bind our fates in rhythm and rhyme.

So I yearn for the day I can feel your breath,
To share in the sunsets, defying all depth;
To wander through mountains, to dance in the
sun,
To script our love story where two hearts are
one.

Until then, I'll weave this tale in my mind,
Where we walk on the shore, futures entwined;
I'll guard us from life's relentless spree,
Nurturing our dreams, you and me, wild and
free.

Elusive Arcady

In dreams of first, my heart did race,
A dance with shadows, a desperate chase.
With Sky and Lily, laughter bright,
Yet blinded by envy, I lost my sight.

Beneath the weight of ambition's claim,
I wore a mask, too proud, too ashamed.
For in the eyes of the cruel and fair,
I sought validation, unaware.

But in that moment, cruel and stark,
I found my truth in a heartless dark.
Where once was joy, now stood despair,
A lesson learned, yet hard to bear.
So listen close, dear souls entwined,

In the race to be first, don't leave love behind.
For every crown that glimmers bright,
Can lead a heart to an endless night.

A whisper grazes through the air,
Of dreams and hopes, both brittle and rare.
In shadows cast by longing's flame,
I chased the echoes of an empty name.

In solitude, I faced my plight,
Though ambition gleamed, it felt so slight.
For in the silence, truths unfurl,
That love outweighs the weight of the world.

With each step taken, each bridge I crossed,
I counted the victories, yet felt the cost.
Amidst the laughter, I lost the song,
Fumbling through the night, where I felt I
belonged.

So take this tale, a fragile thread,
A tapestry woven from dreams unsaid.
In every journey, let kindness reign,
For love's sweet embrace conquers all pain.

And when the shadows bid us stay,
Remember to cherish, to dance, to play.
For in the end, when the dust has cleared,
It's love that remains forever endeared.

Courage Redefined

The one who sought the win, they said,
Where promises of glory bled,
With dreams woven in ambition's thread,
But courage faltered; hope was shed.

Through corridors of quiet pain,
They walked with friends now lost to shame.
The laughter faded, leaving a stain,
In the labyrinth of the heart's disdain.

But in the dark, a voice awoke,
'Choose yourself; don't let them choke,
For in this tale of fire and smoke,
True strength is found when bonds aren't broke'.

So with their pen, on paper wide,
They wrote the truth; their heart confides,
A journey fierce, but now with pride,
To turn the tide, no longer hide.

In each setback, a lesson learned,
Through ashes scattered, brightly burned.
With every tear that touched the ground,
A deeper purpose they had found.

With footsteps bold, they forged ahead,
Not fearing where the heart had led.
For every scar, a story spun,
And courage bloomed; the battle was won.

In shadows cast, their spirit soared,
With every line, their voice restored.
In unity, their strength combined,
To redefine what they would find.

A world reshaped by hearts that bleed,
Through kindness sown, embracing need.
The echoes of despair now fade,
In empathy, true courage is made.

The one who sought the win, they said,
With hopes reborn where dreams are fed.
No longer bound by doubt and dread,
In the tapestry of life, they tread.

Reflections of Regret

Running from shadows, I followed a gleam,
Each dream, now twisted in a shattered seam.
Glory once golden, now dulled by despair,
Reached for the stars, but I lost what was rare.

Every friend faltered, the bonds turned to ash,
Time taught me lessons, my heart's silent crash.
Rivers of memories, they flow through my mind,
Echoes of laughter now bitterly blind.

Glimmers of hope, though faintly they call,
Remnants of courage, though trembling, stand
tall.
Endings are burdens we carry in stride,
Through shadows of sorrow, the spirit must
glide.

Still, through the darkness, a flicker persists,
A spark of defiance, a soul that resists.
With each step forward, a strength yet unknown,
In the heart's quiet depths, a courage is grown.

And though the world may dim and shadows
creep,
A silent vow, the soul shall keep.
To rise above the pain, the loss, the strife,
And claim a future filled with life.

Whispers of Freedom

In shadows cast by silent fears,
Where dreams dissolve and fade with tears,
I wade through nights, fighting monsters bright,
Hating the dark that shuns the light.

My heart, a caged and restless thing,
Desires to soar on freedom's wing,
Yet chains of past and pain entwined,
Keep my spirit tightly bind.

I dance on the edge of hope,
In a realm where fantasies elope;
Each breath a plea to break away,
From haunting echoes of dismay.

But oh, the day the fates collide,
A stranger comes, igniting my stride,
With eyes that pierce through layers of doubt,
Unravelling fears I thought were snuffed out.

A scar remains, but with it comes grace,
The bravest journey to embrace;
For in the light of a gentle gaze,
I find the strength to unearth my days.

The Vow of Rebirth

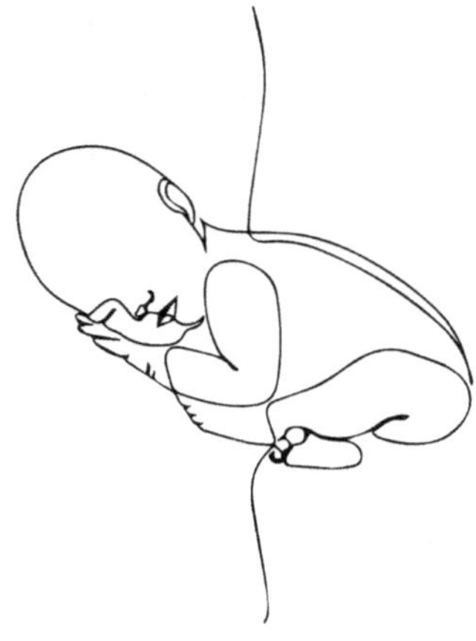

Amidst the labyrinth of thoughts confined,
A whispering hope to courage aligned,
I walk through thickets of despair,
Carrying the weight of a love laid bare.

In a world obscured by shadows and shame,
I'm just a flicker, a fleeting flame,
Yet within the darkness, a spark ignites,
A tender heart that still dares to fight.

I yearn for realms untouched, serene,
Where whispers of life aren't seldom seen;
To push the boundaries of what's deemed real,
And find the solace I desperately feel.

Through the labyrinth of night, I run,
Chasing the warmth of distant suns;
Each heartbeat a promise, a vow to reclaim,
The essence of life I once called my name.

Then in glimmers of time, the curtain falls,
The entrance to new, echoing calls;
With him, the door swings wide and free,
Inviting me to become who I'm meant to be.

A Tapestry of Echoes

In verdant fields where shadows weave,
I cherish what few believe;
A tapestry stitched with threads of sorrow,
Yet amidst the darkness, I dare hope for
tomorrow.

My laughter dances like autumn leaves,
But beneath the surface, my spirit grieves;
For every glance at the world outside,
Hides the ache I dared not confide.

The crude canvas of life's cruel art,
Leaves imprint deep upon my heart;
But fate conspires in untold ways,
In unexpected meetings that set ablaze.

Amongst a crowd, his presence glows,
A gentle strength I never know;
With words like rivers, flowing free,
He breathes life where I struggle to see.

Together we stumble, together we rise,
A connection that shatters my carefully built
lies;
He's the voice that softens the thunderous call,
Helping me break down the insurmountable
wall.